BOND OVER BLOOD

Can the man-made relations feel more like
the 'God-gifted' ones?

H.K. Snowflake

BookLeaf
Publishing

India | USA | UK

Made with ❤ on the BookLeaf Publishing Platform
www.bookleafpub.in
www.bookleafpub.com

Dedication

To all those who suffer in silence
and laugh in crowd; smile
without reason as they receive
the rewards.

Preface

"In the shadows of expectation, where love and pressure entwine, I found my voice in silence."

Growing up as the eldest child, I was moulded by the weight of responsibility and the pursuit of perfection. But beneath the surface, I struggled to find myself, torn between the person I was expected to be and the person I truly am.

"Blood with No Bond" is more than just a collection of poems - it's my story. Growing up, I felt like I was living in the shadow of expectation. My parents' dreams, my family's pride, the weight of being the eldest... it was all so suffocating. I lost myself in the process, trying to fit into the perfect mould they had created for me.

But poetry became my escape, my confidant, my safe space. Through these words, I pour out my heart, my struggles, my doubts. I'm not perfect, and neither are these poems. But they're honest.

This book is for anyone who's ever felt like they're

living a lie, like they're pretending to be someone they're not. It's for those who smile on the outside but cry on the inside. It's for those who feel alone, but aren't.

I hope these words find you, comfort you, and maybe even inspire you to find your own voice.

Acknowledgements

I would like to thank the most to my father, who at all times appreciated my work. By this, I always felt positive about writing next one. I am grateful to God who made me capable of doing all this. Also, thanks to my mother for providing me the atmosphere to be able to write all this.

Thankyou EVERYONE who motivated me for writing more just by uttering a few sweet words. It really meant a lot to me. Lastly, I want to thank my friend for always supporting me at the times I felt the lowest. You are the one who uplifted me when everyone else including me had lost hope.

1. Bad but also the Best

Some people call me a person with no worry,
whereas there are those who think of me in pity.
In hearts of few, I am the source of pleasure,
but for some, selfishness is the quality I carry.
With ones I am close, they keep me like treasure,
while the rest say I am a liability, how uncanny!

Mingled with my mates, child in me is exposed,
with new people, new personality finds its spot.
Who I for real am, this thing haunts me sometimes,
cause for different people, different person in me comes
every time.

If they like it, so do I, no argument in the same,
in one group I stand out, while being the lowest in the
other.
Several places, several layers get attached on my name,
what is my real nature? A question that always bothers.

We are all bad in someone's story,
but we may be the best for someone special.
As in hearts of few, I am the source of pleasure,
While the rest say i am a liability, how uncanny!

2. A King of One is better than Jack of all Trades

What if someday I can't get full score,
not be able to top and be always up to the mark.
Will the love fade away and the hatred will grow?
the things will be the same or the sweet light will get
dark.

Do they love me or is it the abilities of mine,
boast how good I am, but what if I fail sometime.
Will they praise me even when I am at my lowest or
leave me alone due to embarrassment like everybody
else.

Sometimes I think I am not best at anything,
everybody's right, I am just average in everything.
The fear of being hidden in crowd just takes the place of
my mind,
and the reaction of my parents to this is what scares me
all the time.

I think I am never enough to be loved,
its rightly said by my mother.
My mood or sometimes perspective comes,
which ruins all the flowers.

It takes a lot to be someone's favorite one,
that's what I believe.
Never was and what if never become,
that's the thing upon which I grieve.

3. Death: a Cure or Disease

We live only once, could we have one more?
this beautiful creation, enjoyment filled in tons.
Make the best out of it, go on have tours,
play, have fun, don't care who and what you tore.

Heard these many times, but what after that?
once we all will die, did we prepare for it.
Don't be someone vengeful or believe in tit for tat,
have trust that who forgives, sins get cleared bit by bit.

No matter if one is young or as old as time,
end can come anytime, even if you think you are fine.
So why don't we prepare for it, the life after death,
the final destination waiting for all of us ahead.

If one thinks about it, reflects upon the thoughts,
he will realise that death is the permanent cure of pain.
The endless sufferings of this cruel world filled with
people who fought,
for power, money and fulfilling the uncountable desires
like drops of rain.

But know that its only if the person died is pious,
the one with pure intentions, soft heart and for good

who lives.

One who surrenders his will to the Creator and His choice,

after doing good he forgets and if wronged by someone,

then forgives.

4. No Childhood 'Best-friend'

People like watching the moon,
I love the patterns of clouds.
They enjoy and party being in loud,
and I think of finding happiness soon.

Someone asked me about my favourite colour,
in lieu of replying it by mentioning the name of it
I started describing its beauty like a flower,
And how its only pretty in grass green field.

Is it that I can't fathom them,
or I don't want to understand.
Rather than talking I would like to hold a pen,
that's why, I couldn't keep a childhood best friend.

As if time magically stops as soon as I start to write,
I don't have to go, take revenge and fight.
All the pain, the sadness and anger gets healed,
its like after that, the culprit has in front of me kneeled.

5. Will you?

If I give you an ocean,
will you give me a raindrop?
If I gift you a pretty full moon,
will you also admire its craters?

Someday, I will own and share with you a big house,
can you, by your presence, try to make it a loving home?
With poison or petrol if ever I am doused,
would you help me instead of calling me unknown.

If I say that your thoughts are in my mind,
would you rather flee away or give me your time.
And if ever I decide and lend my heart to you,
would you keep it safe and lend me yours too.

6. October

Time flew as it always did, seasons changed, longings the
same,
Many wounded, some healed; majority found newness,
few still in vain.
The month of October has come, everyone cheered,
what if no one remembers? a soul whispered in fear.

Filled with desires, mixed feelings and desperation,
helpless heart conquered by the power of mind.
Does it want assurance or clear cut rejection?
its magic, the messiness, is it found or yet to find.

Letting go of this modern, materialistic world is easier,
its the promise of contentment that's hardest to catch in
race.
Its not the luxurious belongings or to be prettier,
but the affection and care is what the soul really craves.

I hope one day feelings are more valued than man-made
gems,
the time comes when we fall in love and the emotions
never fade.
The words aren't simply said but also deeply meant,

and the patience for the best becomes ultimate solution
to every aid.

9

7. If only I had plot armour...

On a bridge full of roses, she got pricked by its thorns,
while walking barefooted, the delights of her somewhere
gone.
Has it always been like this or someone fetching by a
force,
with no traces left behind, thought of a monster or a
ghost.

Turns out fate plays role in determining what she gets,
petty girl neither has plot armour nor its ever been lent.
Seemed like the door is open, she stepped as she
straightened her back,
empty with no light, the bridge lead into a cul-de-sac.

Her version got blurred and track got dark as she passed,
how foolish to think of herself as main character, oh she
sighed!
The paths are already chosen, that's where she felt
disheartened,
little did she know of creating her own path without
being burdened.

If only she realised fitting in leads to her very own
disguise,

and plot armour isn't a thing, just an illusion with many
ties.
It had always been there, the magic and best of fate
beside,
just a spark of hope and woosh, all the obstacles off our
rides!

8. You can't 'hate' someone unless you love them

With poison filled in mouth of someone in pain,
the teeth got decayed instead of it being spitted on lane.
That very person cried for help, no one ever came,
has it always been like this, every other day felt like a
new game.

With the storm of hatred in someone's soft heart,
broke every piece of it, still no one ever heard.
Is love and hate intertwined? the person then asked,
Late in realising, the soul answered while being
unmasked.

Just like Earth has its own satellite, the pretty moon,
hate has its own, we get it, but a bit later than soon.
Expectation, the eager to do something, are just to name
a few,
being there for ones we love, isn't something that's new.

At times it goes but never comes back to us like thought,
love ignites hatred or we wouldn't have arguments to
sort.
Emotions are brought, these don't come to us without
knock,

we are the ones who always open the door which had
always been locked.

13

9. Need fills, Greed kills

Episode one going on but the next is in our minds,
what, why and how questions— each coming one by one.
Ending makes us realise it was the starting that binds,
whose value only comes when the right time is gone.

Life feels like thrill movies when we don't have enough,
must be a plot which to solve for us is a bit tough.
Spark in heart to achieve is ignited like a blue flame,
keep rushing, no matter from which game we came.

House turns to palace, adding more and more floors,
one black car in garage or new gadgets three or four.
Land became treasure box—having money as its key,
for keeping our fame and names, we called bribe as fee.

On the same land, under one sky,
drinking river water, that's just a lie.
Many are on roads, some are on the beds,
while there are those who have chandeliers
over their heads.

But what if the common water one is content than any other?
there's no status or show off enemies with him to bother.

Being in his own musings, that's all he really needs,
at last it's just his family, he actually has to feed!

15

10. After thunder, sky gets clear.

With every sadness, there comes joy,
just like hardships are followed by ease.
Kids being sabotaged with imposters called toys,
us grown ups get attached with this transient world's
feast.

There comes time when life gives you painful turns,
but at the end of each, a mystic surprise for you awaits.
After every gain, you forget the recently past burns,
flowers bloom and sky gets cleared on the perfect date.

After dark and gloomy night, pleasant and pleasing day
arrives,
the Magical key for its door is hidden in will power.
Hope and patience serve like guards which thrive,
and treasure reaches, in hope of drop comes shower.

Suffering is promise that days will get way better,
time kills but so does heal, just try to give time some
time.
The planner's plan is best, once you'll open the sealed
letter,
in which the author is in love with the reader line to line.

11. I am such a failure

I would love to just die,
if it were the end of all.
I would love to say goodbye,
if it meant for the last call.

But the truth is:
I have no place here to call my home,
no one to say: Oh! they love my soul.
I am just there sitting with faith and hope,
that one day they can be happy, all alone.

Can't I be observant like my mother,
or a bit lovable as the youngest daughter of my father.
Why is it hard to be social like my sister,
'perfect' is a myth, just want to be a bit better.

Everyone says to love yourself,
how to do it, no one ever said.
Guess it's hidden somewhere on a shelf,
got to search it, that's what I read.

The shelf is on top of a point, quite high,
need a tall ladder so as to reach from here.

Found it lying in a crowded space there,
but the ladder of mine was broken, oh I sigh!
18

12. In the end, it's you with you

Have you ever been at your lowest,
like no one is there to help you.
The ones you thought are the best,
turned out to be worst and you had no clue.

I no longer believe in the word 'true friend',
everyone's first priority is themselves.
Mine isn't me, but it is everyone else,
That's why I don't like to ask back the things I lend.

When you give your best and hope all gets well,
however, God has some other thing planned in His head.
Something or the other always comes in the way,
just the slight of it darkens your whole day.

If only I had done this and not that,
the most haunting thoughts I have ever had.
You are arrogant, this is what they call,
the fear of being a failure is the reason of my fall.

13. To love is to live

I close my eyes and all I see is you,
I try to define, but my lips get sealed.
In every emptiness, my mind is full of you,
the wounded parts of mine with you get healed.

Wherever I run, your thought doesn't leave,
before I met you, in love, I didn't believe.
Yes to everything when you are with me,
no interest in anyone, whether he or she.

Making you proud of me has become my new goal,
my heart is now yours cause you put life in my soul.
Thorns turn to petals as you tell me that you are mine,
Tell me all the issues even when you think you are fine.

If you say that there's something that to you seems to
harm,
I will come to you and protect you safely in my arms.
Future without you is like heaven with you light,
I promise to support you in each and every fight.

You say that you are ordinary but look into my eyes,
only then you'll realize where your worth for me lies.
Everything has been better ever-since you entered in my

life,
Now for each day I wait happily instead of holding onto
knife.

To love isn't wrong as they write in many books,
its what you do with that emotion which you feel.
It isn't falling for how charming their face looks,
but about how much for them you really mean.

We love people whose eyes glow with love for us inside,
In front of ones we are real we and no longer try to hide.
An Umbrella can be handed by anyone who cares less,
It's who stands in rain with you out of everybody else.

14. I am the first-born child: of course,

I am the most loved one, that's what everyone says,
the one who is the overachiever in all kinds of race.
The studious, the hard worker, but so do a writer,
the one who's responsible and makes everyone feel
lighter.

Living to fulfil parents' dreams cause the expectations
put are high,
we want you to be the perfect child instead it turned me
quite shy
Being judged and parenting wrong which led to my
disguise,
the childish and the actual soul forced to be buried
inside.

Restrictions have been many and so does the work
assigned,
can't do the things I please as the rules of family are
already defined.
Couldn't go out and be free like every other sibling of
mine,
but still, "why don't you mix up" tag is what fades my
shine.

I would take the whole blame, but won't let you feel
unfair,
I know how it hurts to be felt unfit when you no longer
want to bear...
Bear the loaded investments made and not knowing how
to repay,
so, I just sit and overthink about the time when I will
freely lay.

I wanna grow up and no longer be in faultfinding place
anymore,
just want someone who sees through my flaws without
changing the core.
One who would still love me even if I don't pretend to be
someone else,
as I am sick of acting differently than the way my soul
really tells.

15. Believed in immortality till he died

I thought I have time till it showed me it runs fast,
believed in each advice till I realised it's not for us.
I thought of new future but is has influence of my past,
so all I did is sit back worrying about the created fuss.

I heard one should be grateful till I learned to aspire
more,
with one desire fulfilled next one is waiting at the door.
Promised to never give up before knowing art of letting
go,
always ready to help others till I read it's okay to say a
no.

I heard I should express so I talked about myself,
till I knew an 'over-sharer' is what they call me instead.
Work hard and achieve goals, that's what they said,
it's all about fate when water got over their heads.

Everybody says to enjoy every day
but carelessness takes the side,
be who you are till from criticism you start trying to
hide.
Your present self matters most till first impression comes

in between,

blaming your own self every time till hate ignites within.

They say all this cause they care and want the best for
you,
till the words uttered begin to leave indelible mark in
your mind.
Create your own path unlike stepping on the trodden
one like a blind,
till the road leads to dubiety while you stand there alone
with no clue.

16. Childhood is a concept, not age

One day:

I saw a lady dancing freely as if it was her very first time,
willful and begging for unwanted things as if she was a
child.
In class while all were sitting with no face expression,
she was looking full of herself with no sad impression.

With every clap, she too clapped, for herself to be bit
calmer,
while jumping like a careless hatched, no control on her
actions.
Always had to act like elder one, so now it all felt to be
just normal,
while for others it seemed to be a dark part of some
fiction.

She talked with full passion like it was her first time,
didn't care who's the listener, just yapped like a child.
Her eyes sparked and hoped of getting on every ride,
only to later realize that she's alone in the waiting line.

Well, she sang and laughed at each and every point,
every person criticized about her juvenile behavior.

Escaping from her family, whether it be nuclear or joint,
it's the code of life; she adapted and became believer.

Childhood ...oh she hates it! Thank goodness that it all
ended,
finally, she can have peace and enjoy the life which was
bended.
We really had the best time while she was stuck with no
had,
so, all she does is rewrite the used pages which were
bad...

17. Pretty souls turn places to heaven

People say they want the best for you,
but are the ones who later get jealous of you.
They say they've never met a person as nice as you,
but once you leave, it doesn't take a second for
backbiting to start.

If only people really meant what they said,
and humans received more flowers when alive than
dead.
If only the promises were to be fulfilled and not only
made,
and with time, instead of love, the hatred and anger
would fade.

Oh! How much I wish to live in a world where
only seasons change and not people.
Only things are used and not humans, and love and
happiness
are the ultimate goals, not money and status.

Where can I find a place which is just like a heaven?
not only due to its scenery but because of the angel-like
individuals.

As they say, "what's inside you is always more important than
what's on the outside",
so why don't we beautify our heart and soul rather than
mere body
with materialistic things that hide...
Hide abusive words we use, the gossips we do; the
intentions we have
and the deeds we perform.

What if I say that the ideal world does exist,
you just have to work hard in order to reach it from here.
Will you believe me if I say that only good ones live
there?
and no evil creature is allowed to even get its near!

18. Dear papa,

Let me be honest here, as I don't like to bluff,
your bones getting weak but soul turning tough.
Want you to see the part of my heart that you hold,
your memory is fading, but the care for us is getting
bold.

'Us' includes me, my sister and my sweet mother,
a small group of people, for rest I don't bother.
But you do as besides being my first heroic dad,
you are a good doctor, of what I am proud and glad.

Good here refers to the effort putting person,
a sweet talker and also a patient loving man.
Caring about everyone, spreading kindness in tons,
the 'best' advisor I have got before I start to plan.

Best means the one who always understands others,
instead of jumping to conclusions, talks through the
journey.
Course of river, from which I learn and all the ideas
gather,
You choose the most effective option, without any sort of
hurry.

I always get happy, when I hear from someone saying,
oh! You are like your father, cause that's who I wanna be.
The one who is genius in studies or in playing,
the one who supported me, at the times people flee.

I wish you could hear me when I see you loving mom,
or if only you could know how I feel when you're on
call.
Talking on call with the people in pain or any kind of
sorrow,
the way you treat them even if you have nothing
borrowed.

All I want to say is please don't get old too fast,
I really want to see you in your prime for long.
Everything comes to an end, nothing here lasts,
it's just that I am grateful to the garden where I belong.

Garden, the palace, which with you blooms and I can call
you as my dad,
the place wherein I love peace, but for you I am ready to
hold a knife.
How pleased and thankful I am to have such a loving
person's hand,
I don't know what I did for God to send a treasure like
you in my life.

19. Religion is morality touched by emotions

In a cage, there lived innocent birds, not two but three,
one blue, one green and the other with a blend of the two.
One had sweet voice while the second was taken from zoo,
the third one simply waiting for the time it will be set free.

With each passing hour, they had a little expected fight,
wherein blue couldn't keep itself, thus the anger would ignite.
Taught to hate each other, an ongoing dark conspiracy,
root to turn them weak, it's all master's hidden policy.

Green followed the second one's plan word to word,
for how the two together would kill the third bird.
One day when master came and tried to throw one away,
they shivered and realized it's them against he, in this play.

When all the paths lead to one single destination,
the three birds wanted freedom with no hesitation.
So then they kept their feathers united and together,

as mutual enmity and conflict is what always withers.

Likewise, emotions and desires are building blocks of
humans,
religion gives it meaning, we are no different than the
others.
Purity touches heart when lost connection rebuilds man
to man,
souls get warmth as the deep forgotten love with all it
discovers.

20. Nothing interests me anymore

See! I have got a pretty dress for you,
should I show excitement? I don't know.
Even the little things made me happy too,
but now I can't find that sweet magic anymore.

Painting, baking, playing or singing,
not interested in any as if I have got bored.
Bored with people, with each and every thing,
the pleasures I craved before has now become load.

The desire to be rich and have a luxurious life,
not anymore, just peace and happiness, that's my goal.
The plans I had made and the aims of my life,
have somehow shattered or maybe buried in a hole.

I overthink, I overdo, I over expect from people,
these are my biggest enemies which I can't leave behind.
Confused with what I really want, suddenly someone whispers,
you used to love biology right, now what happened?

My biggest fear is attachments, which never leave my side,

from one person to other, I try hard to hide.
Hide from close bondings, and the dependence on others,
still I find myself stuck in the same cycle that bothers.

If you have a problem I will surely listen with attention,
I will hear your whole story and also weep a little.
I will explore for its solutions as much as possible,
if not, I'll feel guilty, just the way plants shrivel.

I prefer writing over talking so as to express what I feel,
cause there's neither anyone to judge you, nor even to
sigh.
Oh how I wish the soul and life of me to be healed,
and there wouldn't be a thing for which I've to lie.

I am mostly daydreaming, not living in the current time,
they say past or future, but it's imaginary in my case.
You hate over thinkers, they take years to make a
choice?
I guess you haven't met a person yet having more than
one face!

I think I should stop now or I'll continue for more pages,
the more I write, the more I want to continue with the
same.
As if time stops as soon as I start touching the keypad
keys,

cause the more I express, the more is there stored to bleed◻

21. And one day, I met You!

Corners had always been my favourite spot,
I could do anything, even if it's to rot.
My own self was my safest company,
while everybody said that I am not funny.

All my insecurities were believed to define me,
and I had accepted all while sitting on the knee.
Feeling of not worthy, a loser with only flaws,
till I saw you turning every censure into applause.

A bold social daughter was the dream of my mom,
couldn't become, that's why people throw me when I am
torn.
To be someone I am not just to fit in is an ugly norm,
since childhood I had been cursing my soul for to born.

Your coming felt like SA node of my heart,
slowly I started loving imperfections of my soul.
Loving my own self isn't natural but an art,
all my threads scattered which you wove into a whole.

Smile became genuine and laugh a bit merrier,
my eyes got a sparkle which was trapped inside.
Comfort isn't a place, it's a person in my ride,

with whom all joyful moments get extra happier.

I am not pretty, it's your eyes that hold beauty,
my face is just reflection of the light you give off.
You are the rising Sun which blooms me up truly,
completing me by being crests to my troughs.